CONTENTS

INTRODUCTION

This is a story about two very different people. One was named Charles Lutwidge Dodgson. The other was named Lewis Carroll.

Charles Lutwidge Dodgson was a serious person. He was a mathematician who wrote books with titles like *A Syllabus of Plane Algebraical Geometry* and *The Formulae of Plane Trigonometry*, and he spent his entire adult life at Oxford University in England, teaching and writing about advanced mathematics.

Lewis Carroll was a very funny and unpredictable person. He was a writer of stories and poems for children, and his books had titles like *Alice's Adventures in Wonderland, Through the Looking-Glass and What Alice Found There,* and *The Hunting of the Snark.* His stories were full of impossible and ridiculous events. His poems were full of nonsense and silliness. His books portrayed an imaginary world where a child could suddenly grow large or small, where chess pieces talked and argued, where a rabbit worried about being late, where croquet was played with flamingoes instead of mallets, and where a mad hatter gave a tea party for a dormouse.

When newspaper reporters asked Dodgson if he had anything to do with the books written by Lewis Carroll, Dodgson answered that he "neither claimed nor acknowledged any connection with the books not published under his name." But the reporters, and everyone else, knew that Mr. Dodgson and Mr. Carroll were the same person.

Charles Lutwidge Dodgson was born in 1832, the son of a young couple who lived in the small village of Daresbury in the county of Cheshire in England. His father and mother were cousins—in the nineteenth century it was common for cousins to marry each other—and his father was a clergyman who was gifted in mathematics and ancient languages. His childhood was extraordinarily happy. Both his parents were attentive and loving, and his father tutored him in mathematics, languages, and literature. Even as a very small child Charles was interested in mathematics, and once brought a book of complicated formulas to his father and begged, "Please explain!"

As he grew older, Charles began to display the humor and imagination that would later emerge in the works of Lewis Carroll. Charles was his parents' third child and first son; five more girls and three more boys came after. He soon became the chief entertainer for his family. He invented a game in which he and his brothers and sisters pretended to be railway passengers and trains. The rules specified that a passenger who fell off a train had to be run over three times before he could ask for a doctor. As a teenager he made himself the editor and chief writer of magazines that he wrote out by hand for his family. The contents included poems, stories, and jokes that have the same kind of absurdity and comedy he later used in the *Alice* books. In one of the essays he wrote for a family magazine he proved that a stopped clock is more accurate than a clock that falls behind by one minute every day. The stopped clock, after all, tells the correct time twice a day. The other clock never tells the exact time.

At school, and later at Oxford University, Charles showed a special gift for mathematics and logic. After he finished his university studies, his college was so impressed by him that he was given a fellowship that allowed him to live there for the rest of his life. At the age of twenty-four he was appointed the college's chief teacher of mathematics. Around the same time, he began publishing poems and stories in popular magazines. He wanted his real name to be associated with his serious work in mathematics, so he decided to invent a "pen name" that could be printed as the name of the author of his poems and stories. Thus "Lewis Carroll" came into being. At first, the real identity of "Lewis Carroll" was known only to the editors of the magazines he wrote for.

Charles Dodgson, meanwhile, was making his name as a mathematician and as a well-known teacher at Oxford. He was exceptionally tall and exceptionally thin, and he stood exceptionally straight. He was respected for his quiet life, for his unselfish habits, and for a sense of morals that made him strict with himself but forgiving with others. At school he had been well liked for his readiness to defend weaker and younger students when he thought they had been treated unjustly. He was fascinated by up-to-date technology, and was an expert at the new science of photography. He never married, and seems never to have been in love. In later years, however, when he was famous as a writer, he developed a close friendship with a young painter named Gertrude Thomson. Charles met her after he wrote her a letter telling her how much he admired her pictures of fairy stories. He always admired anyone who made things that gave special pleasure to children.

When Charles visited his friends' families, he was always polite to the grownups, but he was most happy among the children. He loved to entertain with games that he invented and stories that he made up while talking to them. These were the same kind of clever and funny stories that he was already writing for magazines, but he seemed especially inspired when he had an audience of live children.

July 4th is not a special day in England, but July 4th, 1862, was a special day for Charles Dodgson and for everyone who loved words and stories. On that day Dodgson and some friends spent the afternoon having a picnic and rowing on the River Thames. The friends included Lorina, Alice, and Edith Liddell (rhymes with "middle"), the three daughters of the dean of his Oxford college. Alice Liddell was ten years old. He had already told many stories to the Liddell children and now they begged him to tell them another. He began by telling a fairy tale about Alice's adventures when she followed a rabbit into a rabbit hole and met many strange and fanciful creatures in a world she had never imagined. Only at the end did she realize that she had been dreaming all along.

Everyone in the boat knew they were hearing an exceptionally good story. The other adult—a clergyman—was so impressed that he asked Dodgson if he had the story already in his mind. Dodgson replied, "I'm inventing as we go along." Alice Liddell was also impressed. She asked Dodgson to write the story down. He said he would think about it, but he didn't seem as if he really wanted to.

Five months later, after Alice asked him a few more times, Dodgson finally began writing down the story that he had invented during that afternoon on the river. He made a copy of the story in his own handwriting (and with pictures that he drew himself), and gave it to Alice Liddell. Its title was *Alice's Adventures Under Ground.* Then, in 1865, he expanded the story and had it published under the title *Alice's Adventures in Wonderland.* The author's name was given on the title page as Lewis Carroll. The book included beautifully detailed pictures by a famous illustrator, John Tenniel, and although hundreds of other artists have illustrated later editions of the book, Tenniel's drawings are almost as famous as the story itself.

Alice in Wonderland (the title is usually shortened to those words) was a great and instant success, and it soon became widely known that Lewis Carroll was really Charles Lutwidge Dodgson. The sequel to the book, *Through the Looking-Glass,* was published in 1871. Other books of prose and verse appeared under Carroll's name, including the long poem *The Hunting of the Snark,* in 1876. When Charles Dodgson died in 1898, he was honored as a mathematician, but mourned as the greatest writer of children's stories in the English language—and probably in any language.

The two *Alice* books were the most famous and most loved of all his work. They were translated into dozens of languages. In the nineteenth century, with Charles's help, the two books were made into a popular stage play. In the twentieth century, they were made into a dozen movie versions. Walt Disney made an animated cartoon of the two *Alice* books that was seen throughout the world.

The poems in the Alice books, and Lewis Carroll's other poems for children, are very different from most children's poems of the nineteenth century. Most pieces prepared for children at the time were written to teach them to behave properly, to obey the rules, and to do as they were told. Lewis Carroll's poems portrayed a world where no one behaved properly, where no one obeyed any rules, and where no one did as he or she was told. Instead of explaining serious and real things, they often used words that didn't refer to anything at all—"Jabberwock," "Snark," "Borogove."

For more than a hundred years, children have found in Lewis Carroll's poems and stories a glimpse of a world of pure enjoyment where everything exists because it gives pleasure, and where everything is valuable because it is itself, not because it serves any useful purpose. At the end of each of the *Alice* books, Alice returns to the ordinary world where sensible adults are just as much in charge as they were before. But simply by visiting Wonderland, merely by journeying through the looking glass, she has learned something just as important, just as valuable, as anything she finds in the world she comes back to.

HOW DOTH THE LITTLE CROCODILE

In this poem, Carroll makes fun of a poem by Isaac Watts, who lived in the 1800s and wrote many poems that were meant to teach children to be diligent and hard-working. The poem begins: "How doth the little busy bee / Improve each shining hour, / And gather honey all the day / From every opening flower!"

How doth the little crocodile
　　Improve his shining tail,
And pour the waters of the Nile
　　On every golden scale!

How cheerfully he seems to grin,
　　How neatly spreads his claws,
And welcomes little fishes in,
　　With gently smiling jaws!

BEAUTIFUL SOUP

Many poets have written poems that praised a beautiful person or the beauties of nature. In this one, Lewis Carroll praises the soup served at dinnertime. (Here he was making fun of a popular song that began "Beautiful star in heav'n so bright.") The poem sounds best when you sing it to a tune that you make up for it.

Beautiful Soup, so rich and green,
Waiting in a hot tureen!
Who for such dainties would not stoop?
Soup of the evening, beautiful Soup!
Soup of the evening, beautiful Soup!
      Beau—ootiful Soo—oop!
      Beau—ootiful Soo—oop!
Soo—oop of the e—e—evening,
      Beautiful, beautiful Soup!

Beautiful Soup! Who cares for fish,
Game, or any other dish?
Who would not give all else for two
Pennyworth only of beautiful Soup?
Pennyworth only of beautiful soup?
      Beau—ootiful Soo—oop!
      Beau—ootiful Soo—oop!
Soo—oop of the e—e—evening,
      Beautiful, beauti—FUL SOUP!

Dainties—*delicious foods.*
Game—*Wild Animals*
   and birds that are hunted in
   order to use as food

'TIS THE VOICE OF THE LOBSTER

Carroll enjoyed making fun of poetry that told children how to behave—a kind of poetry that was common in the 1700s and 1800s. Like "How Doth the Little Crocodile," this poem makes fun of another poem by Isaac Watts, one that many children heard from their parents or teachers. It began, "'Tis the voice of the sluggard; I heard him complain / 'You have waked me too soon, I must slumber again.'"

"'Tis the voice of the Lobster: I heard him declare
'You have baked me too brown, I must sugar my hair!'
As a duck with his eyelids, so he with his nose
Trims his belt and his buttons, and turns out his toes.
When the sands are all dry, he is gay as a lark,
And will talk in contemptuous tones of the Shark:
But, when the tide rises and sharks are around,
His voice has a timid and tremulous sound."

tremulous—*trembling*

FATHER WILLIAM

Again, Carroll is making fun of an earlier, serious poem—this time by Robert Southey, a poet who was very popular in the 1800s. Southey's poem is called "The Old Man's Comforts and How He Gained Them." As you can guess, the old man in Southey's poem was far more sensible (and far less interesting) than the one in Carroll's.

"You are old, Father William," the young man said
    "And your hair has become very white;
And yet you incessantly stand on your head—
    Do you think, at your age, it is right?"

"In my youth," Father William replied to his son,
    "I feared it might injure the brain;
But, now that I'm perfectly sure I have none,
    Why, I do it again and again."

      "You are old," said the youth, "as I mentioned before.
        And have grown most uncommonly fat;
      Yet you turned a back-somersault in at the door—
        Pray, what is the reason of that?"

      "In my youth," said the sage, as he shook his grey locks,
        "I kept all my limbs very supple
      By the use of this ointment—one shilling the box—
        Allow me to sell you a couple?"

You are old," said the youth, "and your jaws are too weak
    For anything tougher than suet;
Yet you finished the goose, with the bones and the beak—
    Pray, how did you manage to do it?"

"In my youth," said his father, "I took to the law,
    And argued each case with my wife;
And the muscular strength, which it gave to my jaw
    Has lasted the rest of my life."

suet—*short for "suet pudding," a pudding made from milk and fat,
    which was often given to sick people because it was easy to digest*

"You are old," said the youth, "one would hardly suppose
    That your eye was as steady as ever;
Yet you balanced an eel on the end of your nose—
    What made you so awfully clever?"

"I have answered three questions and that is enough,"
    Said his father. "Don't give yourself airs!
Do you think I can listen all day to such stuff?
    Be off, or I'll kick you down-stairs!"

BROTHER AND SISTER

Carroll wrote this poem when he was a young man. The "moral" is not one that most brothers or sisters need to learn.

"Sister, sister, go to bed!
Go and rest your weary head."
Thus the prudent brother said.

"Do you want a battered hide,
Or scratches to your face applied?"
Thus his sister calm replied.

"Sister, do not raise my wrath,
I'd make you into mutton broth
As easily as kill a moth!"

The sister raised her beaming eye
And looked on him indignantly
And sternly answered, "Only try!"

Off to the cook he quickly ran,
"Dear Cook, please lend a frying-pan
To me as quickly as you can."

"And wherefore should I lend it you?"
"The reason, Cook, is plain to view.
I wish to make an Irish stew."

"What meat is in that stew to go?"
"My sister'll be the contents!"
                              "Oh!"
"You'll lend the pan to me, Cook?"
                              "No!"

Moral: Never stew your sister.

mutton—*lamb*

15

HUMPTY DUMPTY'S SONG

From start to finish, Humpty Dumpty never manages to tell us exactly what he means. The poem ends in the middle of a sentence, so we never even find out why Humpty Dumpty couldn't turn the handle.

In winter, when the fields are white,
I sing this song for your delight—

In spring, when woods are getting green,
I'll try and tell you what I mean:

In summer, when the days are long,
Perhaps you'll understand the song:

In autumn, when the leaves are brown,
Take pen and ink, and write it down.

I sent a message to the fish:
I told them "This is what I wish."

The little fishes of the sea,
They sent an answer back to me.

The little fishes' answer was
"We cannot do it, Sir, because—"

I sent to them again to say
"It will be better to obey."

The fishes answered, with a grin,
"Why, what a temper you are in!"

I told them once, I told them twice:
They would not listen to advice.

I took a kettle large and new,
Fit for the deed I had to do.

My heart went hop, my heart went thump:
I filled the kettle at the pump.

Then some one came to me and said
"The little fishes are in bed."

I said to him, I said it plain,
"Then you must wake them up again."

I said it very loud and clear:
I went and shouted in his ear.

But he was very stiff and proud:
He said, "You needn't shout so loud!"

And he was very proud and stiff:
He said "I'd go and wake them, if—"

I took a corkscrew from the shelf:
I went to wake them up myself.

And when I found the door was locked,
I pulled and pushed and kicked and knocked.

And when I found the door was shut,
I tried to turn the handle, but—

TWEEDLEDUM AND TWEEDLEDEE

"Tweedledum and Tweedledee" is an old expression meaning (more or less) "two things that are so close to being the same that there is no point in trying to tell them apart." Alice says this poem in her mind when she meets two characters named Tweedledum and Tweedledee in Through the Looking Glass.

Tweedledum and Tweedledee
   Agreed to have a battle;
For Tweedledum said Tweedledee
   Had spoiled his nice new rattle.

Just then flew down a monstrous crow,
   As black as a tar-barrel;
Which frightened both the heroes so,
   They forgot their quarrel.

MATILDA JANE

Matilda Jane is a doll, and the speaker loves it, even though it can't do anything at all. The poem is about a special kind of love—one in which you are loved just because you are you, and not because you are handsome or beautiful or smart or brave or anything else.

Matilda Jane, you never look
At any toy or picture-book:
I show you pretty things in vain—
You must be blind, Matilda Jane!

I ask you riddles, tell you tales,
But all our conversation fails:
You never answer me again—
I fear you're dumb, Matilda Jane!

Matilda, darling, when I call,
You never seem to hear at all:
I shout with all my might and main—
But you're so deaf, Matilda Jane!

Matilda Jane, you needn't mind:
For, though you're deaf, and dumb, and blind,
There's some one loves you, it is plain—
And that is me, Matilda Jane!

dumb—*unable to speak*

THE MOCK TURTLE'S SONG

A dance is—or ought to be—something that everyone can be take part in. In this poem, even a slow-moving snail can join the fun.

"Will you walk a little faster?" said a whiting to a snail,
"There's a porpoise close behind us, and he's treading on my tail.
See how eagerly the lobsters and the turtles all advance!
They are waiting on the shingle—will you come and join the dance?
Will you, won't you, will you, won't you, will you join the dance?
Will you, won't you, will you, won't you, won't you join the dance?

"You can really have no notion how delightful it will be
When they take us up and throw us, with the lobsters, out to sea!"
But the snail replied "Too far, too far!" and gave a look askance—
Said he thanked the whiting kindly, but he would not join the dance.
Would not, could not, would not. could not, could not join the dance.
Would not, could not, would not, could not, could not join the dance.

"What matters it how far we go?" his scaly friend replied.
"There is another shore, you know, upon the other side.
The further off from England the nearer is to France.
Then turn not pale, beloved snail, but come and join the dance.
Will you, won't you, will you, won't you, will you join the dance?
Will you, won't you, will you, won't you, won't you join the dance?"

whiting—*a fish that resembles a cod*
shingle—*in England this means a beach with large stones instead of sand*

THE MOCK TURTLE'S SONG—EARLY VERSION

Carroll wrote this earlier version of the Mock Turtle's song for a draft of Alice in Wonderland *that was not printed until after his death.*

Beneath the waters of the sea
Are lobsters thick as thick can be—
They love to dance with you and me,
    My own, my gentle Salmon!

Chorus:
Salmon come up! Salmon go down!
Salmon come twist your tail around!
Of all the fishes in the sea
    There's none so good as Salmon!

THE WALRUS AND THE CARPENTER

Some years after writing this poem, Carroll decided that the story should end with the Walrus and Carpenter being punished for their cruelty. So, when a musical version of Alice in Wonderland *was being prepared, he wrote some additional lines in which the ghosts of the oysters take revenge on the Walrus and Carpenter by jumping on their chests while they sleep—in other words, by giving them indigestion.*

The sun was shining on the sea,
    Shining with all his might:
He did his very best to make
    The billows smooth and bright—
And this was odd, because it was
    The middle of the night.

The moon was shining sulkily,
    Because she thought the sun
Had got no business to be there
    After the day was done—
"It's very rude of him," she said,
    "To come and spoil the fun!"

The sea was wet as wet could be,
    The sands were dry as dry.
You could not see a cloud, because
    No cloud was in the sky:
No birds were flying overhead—
    There were no birds to fly.

The Walrus and the Carpenter
    Were walking close at hand:
They wept like anything to see
    Such quantities of sand:
"If this were only cleared away,"
    They said, "it would be grand!"

"If seven maids with seven mops
    Swept it for half a year,
Do you suppose," the Walrus said,
    "That they could get it clear?"
"I doubt it," said the Carpenter,
    And shed a bitter tear.

"O Oysters, come and walk with us!"
    The Walrus did beseech.
"A pleasant walk, a pleasant talk,
    Along the briny beach:
We cannot do with more than four,
    To give a hand to each."

The eldest Oyster looked at him,
    But never a word he said:
The eldest Oyster winked his eye,
    And shook his heavy head—
Meaning to say he did not choose
    To leave the oyster-bed.

But four young Oysters hurried up,
    All eager for the treat:
Their coats were brushed, their faces washed,
    Their shoes were clean and neat—
And this was odd, because, you know,
    They hadn't any feet.

Four other Oysters followed them,
　　And yet another four;
And thick and fast they came at last,
　　And more, and more, and more—
All hopping through the frothy waves,
　　And scrambling to the shore.

The Walrus and the Carpenter
　　Walked on a mile or so,
And then they rested on a rock
　　Conveniently low:
And all the little Oysters stood
　　And waited in a row.

"The time has come," the Walrus said,
　　"To talk of many things:
Of shoes—and ships—and sealing wax—
　　Of cabbages—and—kings —
And why the sea is boiling hot—
　　And whether pigs have wings."

"But wait a bit," the Oysters cried,
　　"Before we have our chat;
For some of us are out of breath,
　　And all of us are fat!"
"No hurry!" said the Carpenter.
　　They thanked him much for that.

"A loaf of bread" the Walrus said,
　　"Is what we chiefly need:
Pepper and vinegar besides
　　Are very good indeed—
Now, if you're ready, Oysters dear,
　　We can begin to feed."

"But not on us!" the Oysters cried,
　　Turning a little blue.
"After such kindness, that would be
　　A dismal thing to do!"
"The night is fine," the Walrus said.
　　"Do you admire the view?

"It was so kind of you to come!
   And you are very nice!"
The Carpenter said nothing but
   "Cut us another slice.
I wish you were not quite so deaf—
   I've had to ask you twice!"

"It seems a shame," the Walrus said
   "To play them such a trick.
After we've brought them out so far,
   And made them trot so quick!"
The Carpenter said nothing but
   "The butter's spread too thick!"

"I weep for you," the Walrus said:
   "I deeply sympathize."
With sobs and tears he sorted out
   Those of the largest size,
Holding his pocket-handkerchief
   Before his streaming eyes.

"O Oysters," said the Carpenter,
   "You've had a pleasant run!
Shall we be trotting home again?"
   But answer came there none—
And this was scarcely odd, because
   They'd eaten every one.

THE WHITE RABBIT'S EVIDENCE

During the trial scene in Alice in Wonderland *this poem is used as "evidence." The King says it is "the most important piece of evidence we've heard yet." But Alice says, "I don't believe there's an atom of meaning in it." Alice is probably right.*

They told me you had been to her,
   And mentioned me to him:
She gave me a good character,
   But said I could not swim.

He sent them word I had not gone
   (We know it to be true):
If she should push the matter on,
   What would become of you?

I gave her one, they gave him two,
   You gave us three or more;
They all returned from him to you,
   Though they were mine before.

If I or she should chance to be
   Involved in this affair,
He trusts to you to set them free,
   Exactly as we were.

My notion was that you had been
   (Before she had this fit)
An obstacle that came between
   Him, and ourselves, and it.

Don't let him know she liked them best,
   For this must ever be
A secret, kept from all the rest,
   Between yourself and me.

gave me a good character—*wrote a letter*
   saying that I was honest and could be trusted

JABBERWOCKY

This adventure story doesn't make sense, but it's exciting anyway. Some of the nonsense words are made out of ordinary words. "Slithy" is from "slimy" and "lithe" (flexible). "Frumious" is from "furious" and "fuming." Carroll said that "uffish" reminded him of the way you feel when "the voice is gruffish, the manner roughish, and the temper huffish." Some of the words that look like nonsense are real words that were used very rarely or were no longer used. "Gyre" means "whirl around" (as in "gyrate"). "Whiffling" means "blowing with short puffs." "Beamish" means "shining brightly" or "beaming." Today "chortled" is an ordinary word, meaning a laugh that sounds like a combined chuckle and snort, but Carroll invented the word for this poem.

'Twas brillig, and the slithy toves
   Did gyre and gimble in the wabe:
All mimsy were the borogoves,
   And the mome raths outgrabe.

"Beware the Jabberwock, my son!
   The jaws that bite, the claws that catch!
Beware the Jubjub bird, and shun
   The frumious Bandersnatch!"

He took his vorpal sword in hand:
   Long time the manxome foe he sought—
So rested he by the Tumtum tree,
   And stood awhile in thought.

And, as in uffish thought he stood,
   The Jabberwock, with eyes of flame,
Came whiffling through the tulgey wood,
   And burbled as it came!

One, two! One, two! And through and through
   The vorpal blade went snicker-snack!
He left it dead, and with its head
   He went galumphing back.

"And hast thou slain the Jabberwock?
   Come to my arms, my beamish boy!
O frabjous day! Callooh! Callay!"
   He chortled in his joy.

'Twas brillig, and the slithy toves
   Did gyre and gimble in the wabe:
All mimsy were the borogoves,
   And the mome raths outgrabe.

THE WHITE KNIGHT'S SONG

In the late 1700s, the famous poet William Wordsworth wrote a poem called "Resolution and Independence" in which the speaker asks an old beggar how he manages to live. While the beggar gives him an answer, the speaker thinks about the old man's sufferings and stops listening to his words. So he asks the beggar the same question again. Carroll, like many other readers, thought Wordsworth was being ridiculous, and he is making fun of him here.

I'll tell thee everything I can:
  There's little to relate.
I saw an aged, aged man,
  A-sitting on a gate.
"Who are you, aged man?" I said.
  "And how is it you live?"
And his answer trickled through my head,
  Like water through a sieve.

He said "I look for butterflies
  That sleep among the wheat:
I make them into mutton-pies,
  And sell them in the street.
I sell them unto men," he said,
  "Who sail on stormy seas;
And that's the way I get my bread—
  A trifle, if you please."

But I was thinking of a plan
  To dye one's whiskers green,
And always use so large a fan
  That they could not be seen.
So, having no reply to give
  To what the old man said,
I cried "Come, tell me how you live!"
  And thumped him on the head.

His accents mild took up the tale:
    He said "I go my ways,
And when I find a mountain-rill,
    I set it in a blaze;
And thence they make a stuff they call
    Rowland's Macassar-Oil—
Yet twopence-halfpenny is all
    They give me for my toil."

But I was thinking of a way
    To feed oneself on batter,
And so go on from day to day
    Getting a little fatter.
I shook him well from side to side,
    Until his face was blue:
"Come, tell me how you live," I cried,
    "And what it is you do!"

He said "I hunt for haddocks' eyes
    Among the heather bright,
And work them into waistcoat-buttons
    In the silent night.
And these I do not sell for gold
    Or coin of silvery shine,
But for a copper halfpenny.
    And that will purchase nine.

"I sometimes dig for buttered rolls,
    Or set limed twigs for crabs:
I sometimes search the grassy knolls
    For wheels of Hansom-cabs.
And that's the way" (he gave a wink)
    "By which I get my wealth—
And very gladly will I drink
    Your Honour's noble health."

I heard him then, for I had just
    Completed my design
To keep the Menai bridge from rust
    By boiling it in wine.
I thanked him much for telling me
    The way he got his wealth,
But chiefly for his wish that he
    Might drink my noble health.

And now, if e'er by chance I put
    My fingers into glue,
Or madly squeeze a right-hand foot
    Into a left-hand shoe,
Or if I drop upon my toe
    A very heavy weight,
I weep for it reminds me so
Of that old man I used to know—
Whose look was mild, whose speech was slow
Whose hair was whiter than the snow,
Whose face was very like a crow,
With eyes, like cinders, all aglow,
Who seemed distracted with his woe,
Who rocked his body to and fro.
And muttered mumblingly and low,
As if his mouth were full of dough,
Who snorted like a buffalo—
That summer evening long ago,
    A-sitting on a gate.

aged (pronounced as two syllables)—*old*
rill—*a stream*
Rowland's Macassar-Oil—*a famously sticky hair-oil*
haddock—*a fish somewhat smaller than a cod*
limed twigs—*twigs smeared with a sticky substance, used for catching birds*
Hansom-cabs—*horse-drawn carriages with two wheels*
the Menai bridge—*a large iron bridge in Wales*

A SEA DIRGE

*A dirge is a poem that expresses grief over the death
of someone. Here Carroll is making fun of poems
about the wonders of the sea.*

There are certain things—as, a spider, a ghost,
    The income-tax, gout, an umbrella for three—
That I hate, but the thing that I hate the most
    Is a thing they call the Sea.

Pour some salt water over the floor—
    Ugly I'm sure you'll allow it to be:
Suppose it extended a mile or more,
    That's very like the Sea.

Beat a dog till it howls outright—
    Cruel, but all very well for a spree:
Suppose that he did so day and night,
    That would be like the Sea.

I had a vision of nursery-maids;
    Tens of thousands passed by me—
All leading children with wooden spades,
    And this was by the Sea.

Who invented those spades of wood?
    Who was it cut them out of the tree?
None, I think, but an idiot could—
    Or one that loved the Sea.

It is pleasant and dreamy, no doubt, to float
    With "thoughts as boundless, and souls as free":
But, suppose you are very unwell in the boat,
    How do you like the Sea?

There is an insect that people avoid
    (Whence is derived the verb "to flee").
Where have you been by it most annoyed?
    In lodgings by the Sea.

If you like your coffee with sand for dregs,
    A decided hint of salt in your tea,
And a fishy taste in the very eggs—
    By all means choose the Sea.

30

And if, with these dainties to drink and eat,
  You prefer not a vestige of grass or tree,
And a chronic state of wet in your feet,
  Then—I recommend the Sea.

For I have friends who dwell by the coast—
  Pleasant friends they are to me!
It is when I am with them I wonder most
  That anyone likes the Sea.

They take me a walk: though tired and stiff,
  To climb the heights I madly agree;
And, after a tumble or so from the cliff,
  They kindly suggest the Sea.

I try the rocks, and I think it cool
  That they laugh with such an excess of glee,
As I heavily slip into every pool
  That skirts the cold cold Sea.

gout—*a disease that makes the joints of
  the body very painful*
"thoughts as boundless"—*Carroll is
  quoting from "The Corsair," a poem
  written in the early 1800s by the
  English poet Lord Byron, about a
  fearless hero and his adventures.*

POETA FIT, NON NASCITUR

"Poeta fit, non nascitur" is Latin for "a poet is made, not born." In choosing this title Carroll turned upside down a Latin proverb, "Poeta nascitur, non fit," ("a poet is born, not made"), which means that someone is a poet naturally, and cannot become one through studying. In this poem Carroll is making fun of some of the styles of poetry of his time. One of those styles was called "spasmodic," because it sounded choppy and incomprehensible—like someone having a spasm. Only the first few stanzas of the original long poem are printed here.

"How shall I be a poet?
How shall I write in rhyme:
You told me once 'the very wish
Partook of the sublime.'
Then tell me how! Don't put me off
With your 'another time'!"

The old man smiled to see him,
To hear his sudden sally;
He liked the lad to speak his mind
Enthusiastically;
And thought "There's no hum-drum in him,
Nor any shilly-shally."

"And would you be a poet
Before you've been to school?
Ah, well! I hardly thought you
So absolute a fool.
First learn to be spasmodic—
A very simple rule.

"For first you write a sentence,
And then you chop it small;
Then mix the bits, and sort them out
Just as they chance to fall:
The order of the phrases makes
No difference at all.

"Then, if you'd be impressive,
Remember what I say,
That abstract qualities begin
With capitals alway:
The True, the Good, the Beautiful—
Those are the things that pay!"

32

HORRORS

The title and the opening lines of this poem tell you that it is about horrible things. But when you come across the silly-sounding word "grimmliest," you can guess that the poem won't be horrible from beginning to end.

Methought I walked a dismal place
Dim horrors all around;
The air was thick with many a face,
And black as night the ground.

I saw a monster come with speed,
Its face of grimmliest green,
On human beings used to feed,
Most dreadful to be seen.

I could not speak, I could not fly,
I fell down in that place,
I saw the monster's horrid eye
Come leering in my face!

Amidst my scarcely-stifled groans,
Amidst my moanings deep,
I heard a voice, "Wake! Mr. Jones,
You're screaming in your sleep!"

DREAMLAND

*When he wanted to, Carroll could write
sad and serious poems as well as comic
and nonsensical ones.*

When midnight mists are creeping,
And all the land is sleeping,
Around me tread the mighty dead,
And slowly pass away.

Lo, warriors, saints, and sages,
From out the vanished ages,
With solemn pace and reverend face
Appear and pass away.

The blaze of noonday splendour,
The twilight soft and tender,
May charm the eye: yet they shall die,
Shall die and pass away.

But here, in Dreamland's centre,
No spoiler's hand may enter,
These visions fair, this radiance rare,
Shall never pass away.

I see the shadows falling,
The forms of old recalling;
Around me tread the mighty dead,
And slowly pass away.

sages—*wise persons*

35

THE WHITE QUEEN'S SONG

The White Queen in Through the Looking Glass *says she knows "a lovely riddle—all in poetry—all about fishes." After the White Queen says the riddle-poem, the Red Queen says to Alice, "Take a minute to think about it, then guess." But then everyone gets distracted, and the solution to the riddle is never told in the book.*

"'First, the fish must be caught.'
That is easy: a baby, I think, could have caught it.
'Next, the fish must be bought.'
That is easy: a penny, I think, would have bought it.

'Now cook me the fish!'
That is easy, and will not take more than a minute.
'Let it lie in a dish!'
That is easy, because it already is in it.

'Bring it here! Let me sup!'
It is easy to set such a dish on the table.
'Take the dish-cover up!'
Ah, *that* is so hard that I fear I'm unable!

For it holds it like glue—
Holds the lid to the dish, while it lies in the middle:
Which is easiest to do,
Un-dish-cover the fish, or dishcover the riddle?"

The solution to the riddle is "an oyster."

36

THE HUNTING OF THE SNARK

Like "Jabberwocky," this is a nonsense poem about a great adventure—the hunting of the terrifying Snark, which no one has ever seen. As the poem opens, the crew of the Snark-hunting ship lands on a shore where they hope to find their prey.

"Just the place for a Snark!" the Bellman cried,
  As he landed his crew with care;
Supporting each man on the top of the tide
  By a finger entwined in his hair.

"Just the place for a Snark! I have said it twice:
  That alone should encourage the crew.
Just the place for a Snark! I have said it thrice:
  What I tell you three times is true."

The crew was complete: it included a Boots—
  A maker of Bonnets and Hoods—
A Barrister, brought to arrange their disputes—
  And a Broker, to value their goods.

The list of the crew continues:
There was also a Beaver, that paced on the deck,
  Or would sit making lace in the bow:
And had often (the Bellman said) saved them from wreck
  Though none of the sailors knew how.

There was one who was famed for the number of things
  He forgot when he entered the ship:
His umbrella, his watch, all his jewels and rings,
  And the clothes he had bought for the trip.

About this forgetful character, Carroll writes:
He came as a Baker: but owned, when too late—
  And it drove the poor Bellman half-mad—
He could only bake Bride-cake—for which, I may state,
  No materials were to be had.

The last of the crew needs especial remark,
    Though he looked an incredible dunce:
He had just one idea—but, that one being "Snark,"
    The good Bellman engaged him at once.

The captain of the ship explains to the crew how
to recognize the creature they are seeking:
"Come, listen, my men, while I tell you again
    The five unmistakable marks
By which you may know, wheresoever you go,
    The warranted genuine Snarks.

"Let us take them in order. The first is the taste,
    Which is meagre and hollow, but crisp:
Like a coat that is rather too tight in the waist,
    With a flavour of Will-o'-the-Wisp.

"Its habit of getting up late you'll agree
    That it carries too far, when I say
That it frequently breakfasts at five-o'clock tea,
    And dines on the following day.

"The third is its slowness in taking a jest.
    Should you happen to venture on one,
It will sigh like a thing that is deeply distressed:
    And it always looks grave at a pun.

"The fourth is its fondness for bathing-machines,
    Which it constantly carries about,
And believes that they add to the beauty of scenes—
    A sentiment open to doubt.

"The fifth is ambition. It next will be right
    To describe each particular batch:
Distinguishing those that have feathers, and bite,
    From those that have whiskers, and scratch."

The Bellman adds further details about how to hunt a Snark:
"The rest of my speech" (he exclaimed to his men)
    "You shall hear when I've leisure to speak it,
But the Snark is at hand, let me tell you again!
    'Tis your glorious duty to seek it!

"To seek it with thimbles, to seek it with care;
    To pursue it with forks and hope;
To threaten its life with a railway-share;
    To charm it with smiles and soap!

"For the Snark's a peculiar creature, that won't
    Be caught in a commonplace way.
Do all that you know, and try all that you don't:
    Not a chance must be wasted to-day!"

*The crew eventually finds a Snark, and it turns out to be a
Boojum—but if you want to know about Boojums, you will
need to read the complete poem.*

bellman—*a town crier; someone who rings a bell as he walks
    through the streets making announcements*
boots—*a shoemaker*
barrister—*a lawyer*
Bride-cake—*wedding cake*
will-o'-the-wisp—*a goal that can't be reached, a fantasy*
railway-share—*this strange eighteenth-century invention was a
    box on wheels that could be rolled from the beach into the
    water. While remaining inside it, a lady was able to go into the
    water without being seen in her bathing-costume.*
bathing-machine—*a stock-market share in a railway company*

FACTS

The facts in this poem are surely facts, but not very serious ones.

Were I to take an iron gun,
And fire it off towards the sun;
I grant 'twould reach its mark at last,
But not till many years had passed.

But should that bullet change its force,
And to the planets take its course,
'Twould never reach the nearest star,
Because it is so very far.

RULES AND REGULATIONS

As you would expect from Lewis Carroll, these rules and regulations aren't very hard to obey, even if the words seem hard to understand.

A short direction
To avoid dejection,
By variations
In occupations,
And prolongation
Of relaxation,
And combinations
Of recreations,
And disputation
On the state of the nation
In adaptation
To your station,
By invitations
To friends and relations,
By evitation
Of amputation,
By permutation
In conversation,
And deep reflection
You'll avoid dejection.

Learn well your grammar,
And never stammer,
Write well and neatly,
And sing most sweetly,
Be enterprising,
Love early rising,
Go walk of six miles,
Have ready quick smiles,
With lightsome laughter,
Soft flowing after.

Drink tea, not coffee;
Never eat toffy.
Eat bread with butter.
Once more, don't stutter.
Don't waste your money,
Abstain from honey.
Shut doors behind you,
(Don't slam them, mind you.)
Drink beer, not porter.
Don't enter the water
Till to swim you are able.
Sit close to the table.
Take care of a candle.
Shut a door by the handle,
Don't push with your shoulder
Until you are older.
Lose not a button.
Refuse cold mutton.
Starve your canaries.
Believe in fairies.
If you are able,
Don't have a stable
With any mangers.
Be rude to strangers.

Moral: Behave.

evitation—*avoidance*
permutation—*change, variation*
porter—*a dark brown beverage some-
     thing like beer*

THE MAD GARDENER'S SONG

Carroll wrote a very long novel in two parts called Sylvie and Bruno, *about two children and their nonsensical adventures. Every now and then Sylvie and Bruno meet an eccentric gardener, and each time they meet him he sings one of the stanzas of this song. Here are a few of the stanzas.*

He thought he saw an Elephant,
　　That practised on a fife:
He looked again, and found it was
　　A letter from his wife.
"At length I realise," he said,
　　"The bitterness of Life."

He thought he saw a Buffalo
　　Upon the chimney-piece:
He looked again, and found it was
　　His Sister's Husband's Niece.
"Unless you leave this house," he said,
　　"I'll send for the Police!"

He thought he saw a Rattlesnake
　　That questioned him in Greek:
He looked again, and found it was
　　The Middle of Next Week.
"The one thing I regret," he said,
　　"Is that it cannot speak!"

He thought he saw a Banker's Clerk
　　Descending from the bus:
He looked again, and found it was
　　A Hippopotamus:
"If this should stay to dine," he said,
　　"There won't be much for us!"

He thought he saw a Kangaroo
    That worked a coffee-mill:
He looked again, and found it was
    A Vegetable-Pill.
"Were I to swallow this," he said,
    "I should be very ill!"

He thought he saw a Coach-and-Four
    That stood beside his bed:
He looked again, and found it was
    A Bear without a Head.
"Poor thing," he said, "poor silly thing!
    It's waiting to be fed!"

He thought he saw an Albatross
    That fluttered round the lamp:
He looked again, and found it was
    A Penny-Postage-Stamp.
"You'd best be getting home," he said:
    "The nights are very damp!"

LADY MURIEL'S SONG

Lady Muriel is a character in Sylvie and Bruno *who says that the only songs she can sing are "desperately sentimental" and asks her listeners, "Are your tears all ready?" But her song has a happy ending, after all.*

There be three Badgers on a mossy stone,
   Beside a dark and covered way:
Each dreams himself a monarch on his throne,
                And so they stay and stay—
Though their old Father languishes alone,
          They stay, and stay, and stay.

There be three Herrings loitering around,
   Longing to share that mossy seat:
Each Herring tries to sing what she has found
           That makes Life seem so sweet.
Thus, with a grating and uncertain sound,
          They bleat, and bleat, and bleat.

The Mother-Herring, on the salt sea-wave,
   Sought vainly for her absent ones:
The Father-Badger, writhing in a cave,
           Shrieked out "Return, my sons!
You shall have buns," he shrieked, "if you'll behave!
          Yea, buns, and buns, and buns!"

"I fear," said she, "your sons have gone astray?
   My daughters left me while I slept."
"Yes'm," the Badger said: "it's as you say."
         "They should be better kept."
Thus the poor parents talked the time away,
        And wept, and wept, and wept.

The Badgers did not care to talk to Fish:
   They did not dote on Herrings' songs:
They never had experienced the dish
          To which that name belongs:
"And oh, to pinch their tails," (this was their wish,)
        "With tongs, yea, tongs, and tongs!"

"And are not these the Fish," the Eldest sighed,
   "Whose Mother dwells beneath the foam?"
"They *are* the Fish!" the Second one replied.
        And they have left their home!"
"Oh wicked Fish," the Youngest Badger cried,
        "To roam, yea, roam, and roam!"

Gently the Badgers trotted to the shore—
   The sandy shore that fringed the bay:
Each in his mouth a living Herring bore—
        Those aged ones waxed gay:
Clear rang their voices through the ocean's roar,
        "Hooray, hooray, hooray!"

TWINKLE, TWINKLE, LITTLE BAT

Carroll made fun of many serious poems. But he could make fun of silly poems too.

Twinkle, Twinkle, little bat!
How I wonder what you're at!
Up above the world you fly,
Like a tea-tray in the sky.

A BOAT, BENEATH A SUNNY SKY

This poem appears on the last page of Through the Looking Glass. *If you read the first letter of each line, from the first line to the last, they spell out the name of the original Alice, Alice Pleasance Liddell.*

A boat, beneath a sunny sky
Lingering onward dreamily
In an evening of July—

Children three that nestle near,
Eager eye and willing ear,
Pleased a simple tale to hear—

Long has paled that sunny sky:
Echoes fade and memories die:
Autumn frosts have slain July.

Still she haunts me, phantomwise,
Alice moving under skies
Never seen by waking eyes.

Children yet, the tale to hear,
Eager eye and willing ear,
Lovingly shall nestle near.

In a Wonderland they lie,
Dreaming as the days go by,
Dreaming as the summers die:

Ever drifting down the stream—
Lingering in the golden gleam—
Life, what is it but a dream?

phantomwise—
like a ghost or
phantom

INDEX